OCT 2011

Physical
Science

The Power of Energy

by Rebecca Weber

CAPSTONE PRESS
a capstone imprint

Pebble Plus is published by Capstone Press,
151 Good Counsel Drive, P.O. Box 669, Mankato, Minnesota 56002.
www.capstonepub.com

Books published by Capstone Press are manufactured with paper
containing at least 10 percent post-consumer waste.

Library of Congress Cataloging-in-Publication Data
Weber, Rebecca.
  The power of energy / by Rebecca Weber.
    p. cm. — (Pebble plus. Physical science)
  Includes bibliographical references and index.
  ISBN 978-1-4296-6605-3 (library binding)
  1. Power resources—Juvenile literature. I. Title.
  TJ163.23.W433 2011
  621.042—dc22   2010034311

Summary: Simple text and color photographs introduce kinds of energy, including wind power, water power, and solar
power.

Editorial Credits
Gillia Olson, editor; Veronica Correia, designer; Eric Gohl, media researcher; Laura Manthe, production specialist

Photo Credits
AP Images/College of Wooster, Matt Dilyard, cover
Capstone Studio/Karon Dubke, 20–21 (all)
Shutterstock/Duncan Gilbert, 9; Eric Gevaert, 1; GorillaAttack, 11; John Brueske, 17; Scott Prokop, 19; slavcic, 13;
    Tomasz Szymanski, 5; T.W. van Urk, 15; Yellowj, 7

Note to Parents and Teachers

The Physical Science series supports national standards related to physical science. This
book describes and illustrates energy. The images support early readers in understanding
the text. The repetition of words and phrases helps early readers learn new words. This book
also introduces early readers to subject-specific vocabulary words, which are defined in the
Glossary section. Early readers may need assistance to read some words and to use the Table of
Contents, Glossary, Read More, Internet Sites, and Index sections of the book.

Printed in the United States of America in North Mankato, Minnesota.
092010
005933CGS11

Table of Contents

What Is Energy?

For breakfast you ate a waffle
and drank a glass of milk.
Later this food will give you
the energy to swing a bat.
Energy is the ability to do work.

Your body isn't the only

thing that needs energy.

Energy heats your home.

It makes trucks and cars go.

Energy comes in many forms.

Solar Energy

Long ago, people learned that the sun was powerful. They built their homes so the sun could keep them warm in winter.

Today people still use the sun's energy. They collect solar energy with solar panels to create electricity. Electricity powers your TV and computer.

Wind Power

Long ago, people used wind to turn windmills. The mills pumped water out of wells. People also used wind to push sailboats across the water.

Today people still use
wind energy. When wind
turns modern windmills,
it makes electricity
for people's homes.

Water Power

People have used river water to travel for thousands of years. Rushing water also turned water wheels. The wheels then moved stones to grind corn.

Water Wheel

Today people still use energy from water. It's called hydroelectric power. In dams moving water turns turbines to make electricity.

Capture Solar Energy

What You Need

- a bright, sunny window
- a black piece of cloth

1 Feel the black cloth. Remember how hot or cold it feels. Then put the black cloth in a sunny place next to the window.

2 Let it stay there for 10 minutes.

Take the cloth back to your desk.

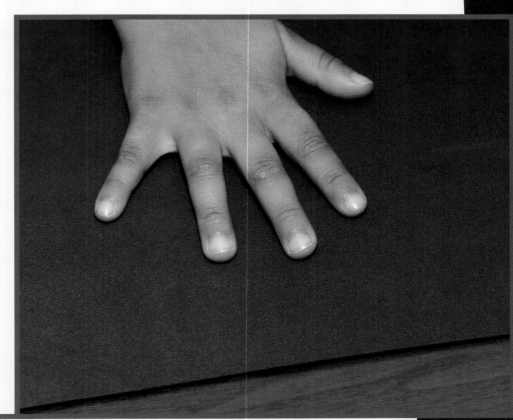

Feel the cloth.
It's warmer.
It's giving off
solar energy.

Glossary

dam—something that stops water from flowing, causing it to back up and make a pool

electricity—a form of energy caused by the movement of very tiny particles

grind—to crush something into a powder

hydroelectric power—energy that is made by flowing water and turned into electricity

solar—having to do with the sun

turbine—an engine powered by steam, water, or gas; the steam or gas moves through the blades of a fanlike device and makes it turn

well—a deep hole drilled to get to water

windmill—a wind-powered machine used to grind grain, pump water, or make electricity

Read More

Gaarder-Juntti, Oona. *What in the World Is Green Energy?* Going Green. Edina, Minn.: ABDO Pub. Company, 2011.

Hord, Colleen. *Clean and Green Energy.* Green Earth Science. Vero Beach, Fla.: Rourke Pub. LLC, 2011.

Mayer, Lynne. *Newton and Me.* Mount Pleasant, S.C.: Sylvan Dell Pub., 2010.

Internet Sites

FactHound offers a safe, fun way to find Internet sites related to this book. All of the sites on FactHound have been researched by our staff.

Here's all you do:

Visit *www.facthound.com*

Type in this code: 9781429666053

Check out projects, games and lots more at
www.capstonekids.com

Index

Word Count: 187
Grade: 1
Early-Intervention Level: 22